Breaking Open

Other books by Muriel Rukeyser

BREAKING
OPEN

Muriel Rukeyser

Random House   New York

Library of Congress Cataloging in Publication Data

Rukeyser, Muriel, 1913-
  Breaking open.
  Poems.
  I. Title.
PS3535.U4B7   811'.5'2   73-5045
ISBN 0-394-48696-X (hardbound)
ISBN 0-394-70981-0 (paperbound)

  My thanks to the following publications and to their editors.
Poems in this book first appeared: "Looking at Each Other" in *New
York Quarterly*; "Despisals" in *Antaeus*; "This Morning in *Mademoi-
selle*; "Ballad of Orange and Grape" in *New American Review*; "A
Simple Experiment" in *New American Review*; "The Writer" in
The World of Translation (P.E.N.); "Wherever," "Fields Where
We Slept" in *29 Poems* by Muriel Rukeyser (Rapp & Whiting/André
Deutsch, London); "All the Little Animals," "After Melville" in *Poetry
Review* (London); "To Be a Jew" in the Reform Jewish prayerbook,
Service of the Heart (London), and *Beast in View* (Doubleday) and
Selected Poems of Muriel Rukeyser (New Directions); "Fire" and
"City of Paradise" in *Mundus Artium*; "The Running of the Grunion"
in *Ararat*; "Iris" (part 1) in *The New Yorker*, the entire poem in
29 Poems; "In the Underworld" in *Transatlantic Review*; "Bringing"
in *Green Flag* (City Light Books); "Next" in *Stony Brook Review*;
"Flying to Hanoi" in *American Report*; "Waiting for Icarus" in
Vogue; "It Is There" in *American Review*.
  The group of poems, "Searching/Not Searching" in *New York
Quarterly*.
  From the poem "Breaking Open," parts 19 and 20 in *Poetry
Magazine*; parts 8, 11, 12, 13 in *The Nation*; first part of 1, 2, 10, 17
in *Antaeus*.

Manufactured in the United States of America
9 8 7 6 5 4 3 2
First Edition

Contents

[v

II Orange and Grape

III   Northern Poems (translated with Paul Radin)

IV   Breaking Open

Searching/Not Searching

This Morning

Waking this morning,
a violent woman in the violent day
Laughing.
                    Past the line of memory
along the long body of your life
in which move childhood, youth, your lifetime of touch,
eyes, lips, chest, belly, sex, legs, to the waves of the sheet.
I look past the little plant
on the city windowsill
to the tall towers bookshaped, crushed together in greed,
the river flashing flowing corroded,
the intricate harbor and the sea, the wars, the moon, the
    planets, all who people space
in the sun visible invisible.
African violets in the light
breathing, in a breathing universe.   I want strong peace,
    and delight,
the wild good.
I want to make my touch poems:
to find my morning, to find you entire
alive moving among the anti-touch people.

                    I say across the waves of the air to you:
today once more
I will try to be non-violent

one more day
this morning, waking the world away
in the violent day.

Despisals

In the human cities, never again to
despise the backside of the city, the ghetto,
or build it again as we build the despised
backsides of houses.   Look at your own building.
You are the city.

Among our secrecies, not to despise our Jews
(that is, ourselves) or our darkness, our blacks,
or in our sexuality   wherever it takes us
and we now know we are productive
too productive, too reproductive
for our present invention — never to despise
the homosexual who goes building another

with touch   with touch   (not to despise any touch)
each like himself, like herself each.
You are this.
                            In the body's ghetto
never to go despising the asshole
nor the useful shit that is our clean clue
to what we need.   Never to despise
the clitoris in her least speech.

Never to despise in myself what I have been taught
to despise.   Not to despise the other.
Not to despise the *it*.   To make this relation
with the it : to know that I am it.

What Do We See?

When they're decent about women, they're frightful about
  children,
When they're decent about children, they're rotten about
  artists,
When they're decent about artists, they're vicious about
  whores,
      What do we see?   What do we not see?

When they're kind to whores, they're death on communists,
When they respect communists, they're foul to bastards,
When they're human to bastards, they mock at
  hysterectomy—
      What do we see?   What do we not see?

When they're decent about surgery, they bomb the
  Vietnamese,
When they're decent to Vietnamese, they're frightful to
  police,
When they're human to police, they rough up lesbians,
      What do we see?   What do we not see?

When they're decent to old women, they kick homosexuals,
When they're good to homosexuals, they can't stand drug
  people,
When they're calm about drug people, they hate all
  Germans,

What do we see?   What do we not see?

Cadenza for the reader

When they're decent to Jews, they dread the blacks,
When they know blacks, there's always something :
  roaches
And the future and children and all potential.   Can't
  stand themselves
        Will we never see?   Will we ever know?

Looking at Each Other

Yes, we were looking at each other
Yes, we knew each other very well
Yes, we had made love with each other many times
Yes, we had heard music together
Yes, we had gone to the sea together
Yes, we had cooked and eaten together
Yes, we had laughed often day and night
Yes, we fought violence and knew violence
Yes, we hated the inner and outer oppression
Yes, that day we were looking at each other
Yes, we saw the sunlight pouring down
Yes, the corner of the table was between us
Yes, bread and flowers were on the table
Yes, our eyes saw each other's eyes
Yes, our mouths saw each other's mouth
Yes, our breasts saw each other's breasts
Yes, our bodies entire saw each other
Yes, it was beginning in each
Yes, it threw waves across our lives
Yes, the pulses were becoming very strong
Yes, the beating became very delicate
Yes, the calling   the arousal
Yes, the arriving   the coming
Yes, there it was for both entire
Yes, we were looking at each other

Desdichada

I.

For that you never acknowledged me, I acknowledge
the spring's yellow detail, the every drop of rain,
the anonymous unacknowledged men and women.
The shine as it glitters in our child's wild eyes,
one o'clock at night.   This river, this city,
the years of the shadow on the delicate skin
of my hand, moving in time.
Disinherited, annulled, finally disacknowledged
and all of my own asking.   I keep that wild dimension
of life and making and the spasm
upon my mouth as I say this word of acknowledge
to you forever.   *Ewig*.   Two o'clock at night.

II.

While this my day and my people are a country not yet born
it has become an earth I can
acknowledge.   I must.   I know what the
disacknowledgment does.   Then I do take you,
but far under consciousness, knowing
that under under flows a river wanting
the other : to go open-handed in Asia,
to cleanse the tributaries and the air, to make for making,
to stop selling death and its trash, pour plastic down
  men's throats,

to let this child find, to let men and women find,
knowing the seeds in us all.   They do say Find.
I cannot acknowledge it entire.   But I will.
A beginning, this moment, perhaps, and you.

III .

Death flowing down past me, past me, death
marvelous, filthy, gold,
in my spine in my sex upon my broken mouth
and the whole beautiful mouth of the child;
shedding power over me
death
if I acknowledge him.
Leading me
in my own body
at last in the dance.

Voices

Voices of all our voices, running past an imagined race.
Pouring out of morning light, the pouring mists of Mil
   Cumbres.
Out of the poured cities of our world.
Out of the black voice of one child
Who sleeps in our poverty and is dreaming.

The child perceives and the cycles are fulfilled.

Cities being poured; and war-fire over the poor.
Mist over the peak.
One child in his voices, many voices.
The suffering runs past the end of the racing
Making us run the next race. The child sleeps.
Lovers, makers, this child, enter into our voices.
Speak to the child.   Now something else is waking:
The look of the lover, the rebel and learning look,
The look of the runner just beyond the tape, go into
The child's look at the world.   In all its voices.

Aug. 26, 1968—by invitation for the Olympics. For Otto Boch,
who came to Barcelona July 1936 to run in the Anti-fascist Olympics.

Fire

(after Vicente Aleixandre)

The fire entire
                    withholds
passion.
          Light alone!
Look   —
          it leaps up pure
to lick at heaven,
while all the wings
fly through.
               It won't burn!
And man?
          Never.
                    This fire
is still
free of you, man.

Light, innocent light.

And you, human:
better never be born.

Waiting for Icarus

He said he would be back and we'd drink wine together
He said that everything would be better than before
He said we were on the edge of a new relation
He said he would never again cringe before his father
He said that he was going to invent full-time
He said he loved me that going into me
He said was going into the world and the sky
He said all the buckles were very firm
He said the wax was the best wax
He said Wait for me here on the beach
He said Just don't cry

I remember the gulls and the waves
I remember the islands going dark on the sea
I remember the girls laughing
I remember they said he only wanted to get away from me
I remember mother saying : Inventors are like poets,
                              a trashy lot
I remember she told me those who try out inventions are
   worse
I remember she added : Women who love such are the
   worst of all

I have been waiting all day, or perhaps longer.
I would have liked to try those wings myself.
It would have been better than this.

from City of Paradise

(after Vicente Aleixandre)

To my city of Malaga

There was I led by a maternal hand.
Accident of flowering grillwork, that sad guitar
singing a song abruptly held in time;
the night went quiet, more quieted the lover,
the moon forever, in interrupted light.

One breath of eternity could destroy you,
prodigious city, moment emerged from a god's mind.
According to a dream man lives and does not live,
eternally gleaming like a breath of heaven.

Gardens, flowers. The sea breathing, someone's arm
stretched gasping to the city swinging from peak to gulf,
white in air, have you seen birds in the wind held by gusts
and not rising in flight?   O city not of earth!

By what maternal hand was I borne lightly
along your weightless streets. Barefoot by day.
Barefoot by night.   Big moon.   Pure sun.
The sky was you, city who lived in the sky.
You took flight in the sky with open wings.

The Question

Mother and listener she is, but she does not listen.
I look at her profile as I ask, the sweet blue-grey of eye
going obdurate to my youth as I ask the first grown sexual
question.   She cannot reply.
And from then on even past her death, I cannot fully
have language with my mother, not as daughter
and mother through all the maze and silences
of all the turnings.
Until my own child grows and asks, and until
I discover what appalled my mother long before, discover
who never delivered her, until their double weakness and
strength in myself
rouse and deliver me from that refusal.
I threw myself down on the pine-needle evening.
Although that old ancient poem never did come to me,
not from you, mother,
although in answer you did only panic, you did only grieve,
and I went silent alone, my cheek to the red pine-needle
earth, and although it has taken me all these years
and sunsets to come to you, past the dying, I know,
I come with my word alive.

In Her Burning

The randy old
woman said
Tickle me up
I'll be
dead very soon—
Nothing will
touch me then
but the clouds
of the sky
and the bone-
white light
off the moon
Touch me
before I go
down
among the bones
My dear one
alone
to the night   —
I said
I know I know
But all I know
tonight
Is that the sun
and the moon
they burn

with the one
one light.

In her burning
signing
what does the
white moon say?
The moon says
The sun
is shining.

Rondel

Now that I am fifty-six
Come and celebrate with me —

What happens to song and sex
Now that I am fifty-six?

They dance, but differently,
Death and distance in the mix;
Now that I'm fifty-six
Come and celebrate with me.

More Clues

Mother, because you never spoke to me
I go my life, do I, searching in women's faces
the lost word, a word in the shape of a breast?

Father, because both of you never touched me
do I search for men building space on space?
There was no touch, both my hands bandaged close.

I come from that, but I come far, to touch to word.
Can they reach me now, or inside out in a universe
of touch, of speech is it? somewhere in me, clues?

Myth

Long afterward, Oedipus, old and blinded, walked the
roads.   He smelled a familiar smell.   It was
the Sphinx.   Oedipus said, "I want to ask one question.
Why didn't I recognize my mother?"   "You gave the
wrong answer," said the Sphinx.   "But that was what
made everything possible," said Oedipus.   "No," she said.
"When I asked, What walks on four legs in the morning,
two at noon, and three in the evening, you answered,
Man.   You didn't say anything about woman."
"When you say Man," said Oedipus, "you include women
too. Everyone knows that."   She said, "That's what
you think."

Searching / Not Searching

> Responsibility is to
> use the power to respond.
> —*after* Robert Duncan

1.

What kind of woman goes searching and searching?
Among the furrows of dark April, along the sea-beach,
in the faces of children, in what they could not tell;
in the pages of centuries —
for what man? for what magic?

In corridors under the earth, in castles of the North,
among the blackened miners, among the old
I have gone searching.
The island-woman told me, against the glitter of sun
on the stalks and leaves of a London hospital.
I searched for that Elizabethan man,
the lost discoverer, the servant of time;
and that man forgotten for belief, in Spain,
and among the faces of students, at Coventry,
finding and finding in glimpses. And at home.
Among the dead I too have gone searching,
a blue light in the brain.
Suddenly I come to these living eyes,
I a live woman look up at you this day
I see all the colors in your look.

2. MIRIAM : THE RED SEA

High above shores and times,
I on the shore
forever and ever.
Moses my brother
has crossed over
to milk, honey,
that holy land.
Building Jerusalem.
I sing forever
on the seashore.
I do remember
horseman and horses,
waves of passage
poured into war,
all poured into journey.
My unseen brothers
have gone over;
chariots
deep seas under.
I alone stand here
ankle-deep
and I sing, I sing,
until the lands
sing to each other.

3. FOR DOLCI

Angel of declaring, you opened before us walls,
the lives of children, water as power.
To control the water is to control our days,
to build a dam is to face the enemy.

We will form a new person who will step forward,
he it is, she it is, assumes full life,
fully responsible. We will bring all the children,
they will decide together.

We will ask these children : what is before you?
They will say what they see.
They will say what they don't see.
Once again we breathe in discovery.

A man, a woman,
will discover
we are each other's sources.

4. CONCRETE

They are pouring the city:
they tear down the towers,
grind their lives,
laughing tainted, the river
flows down to tomorrow.

They are setting the forms,
pouring the new buildings.
Our days pour down.
I am pouring my poems.

5. BRECHT'S GALILEO

Brecht saying : Galileo talking astronomy
Stripped to the torso, the intellectual life
Pouring from this gross man in his nakedness.

Galileo, his physical contentment
Is having his back rubbed by his student; the boy mauls;
The man sighs and transforms it; intellectual product!

Galileo spins a toy of the earth around
The spinning sun; he looks at the student boy.
Learning is teaching, teaching is learning.
Galileo
Demonstrates how horrible is betrayal,
Particularly on the shore of a new era.

6. READING THE *KIEU*

There was always a murder within another murder.
Red leaves and rosy threads bind them together.
The hero of Vietnam's epic is a woman
and she has sold herself to save her father.

Odor of massacres spread on the sky.
Loneliness, the windy, dusty world.
The roads crowded with armor and betrayal.
Mirror of the sun and moon, this land,

in which being handed to soldiers is the journey.
Shame, disgrace, change of seas into burnt fields.
Banners, loudspeakers, violation of each day,
everything being unjust. But she does save him,
and we find everything in another way.

7. THE FLOOR OF OCEAN

Sistine Chapel

Climbing the air, prophet beyond prophet
leaning upon creation backward to the first
creation the great spark of night
breathing sun energy   a gap between finger-tips
across all of space or nothing, infinity.

But beyond this, with this, these
arms raising reaching wavering
as from the floor of ocean
wavering showing swaying like sea-plants
pointing straight up closing the gap between
continual creation and the daily touch.

8. H. F. D.

From you I learned the dark potential
theatres of the acts of man holding
on a rehearsal stage   people and lights.
You in your red hair ran down the darkened
aisle, making documents and poems
in their people form the play.

Hallie it was from you I learned this:
you told the company in dress-rehearsal
in that ultimate equipped building   what they lacked:
among the lighting, the sight-lines, the acoustics,
the perfect revolving stage, they lacked only one thing
the most important thing.   It would come tonight:
The audience   the response

Hallie I learned from you this summer, this
Hallie I saw you lying all gone to bone
the tremor of bone   I stroked the head all sculpture
I held the hands of birds   I spoke to the sealed eyes
the soft live red mouth of a red-headed woman.
I knew Hallie then I could move without answer,
like the veterans for peace, hurling back their medals
and not expecting an answer from the grass.
You taught me this in your dying, for poems and theatre
and love and peace-making that living and my love

are where response and no-response
meet at last, Hallie, in infinity.

9. THE   ARTIST   AS   SOCIAL   CRITIC

They have asked me to speak in public
and set me a subject.

I hate anything that begins : the artist as . . .
and as for "social critic"
at the last quarter of the twentieth century
I know what that is:

late at night, among radio music
the voice of my son speaking half-world away
coming clear on the radio into my room
out of blazing Belfast.

Long enough for me to walk around
in that strong voice.

10. THE   PRESIDENT   AND   THE   LASER   BOMB

He speaks in a big voice through all the air
saying : we have made strength,
we have made a beginning,
we will have lasting peace.

Something shouts on the river.

All night long the acts speak:
the new laser bomb falls impeccably
along the beam of a strict light
finding inevitably a narrow footbridge
in Asia.

11. NOT   SEARCHING

What did I miss as I went searching?
What did I not see?
I renounce all this regret.
Now I will make another try.

One step and I am free.

When it happens to us again and again,
sometimes we know it for we are prepared
but to discover, to live at the edge of things,
to fall out of routine into invention
and recognize at the other edge of ocean
a new kind of man   a new kind of woman
walking toward me into the little surf.
This is the next me   and the next child
daybreak in continual creation.
Dayray we see, we say,
we sing what we don't see.

Picasso saying : I don't search, I find!

And in us our need, the traces of the future,
the egg and its becoming.

I come to you searching and searching.

12. THE   QUESTION

After this crisis,
nothing being conquered,
the theme is set:

to move with the forces,

how to go on
from the moment that
changed our life,

the moment of revelation,

proceeding from the crisis,
from the dream,
and not from the moment
of sleep before it?

✻

13.

Searching/not searching.   To make closeness.
For if this communication was the truth,
then it was this communication itself
which was the value to be supported.

And for this communication to endure,
men and women must move freely.   And to make
this communication renew itself always
we must renew justice.
And to make this communication
lasting, we must live to eliminate
violence and the lie.

Yes, we set the communication
we have achieved
against the world of murder.

Searching/not searching.

after Camus, 1946

✿

14.

What did I see? What did I not see?
The river flowing past my window.
The night-lit city. My white pointed light.
Pieces of a world away
within my room.

Unseen and seen, the bodies within my life.
Voices under the leaves of Asia,
and America, in sex, in possibility.
We are trying to make, to let our closeness be made,
not torn apart tonight by our dead skills.

The shadow of my hand.
The shadow of the pen.
Morning of the day we reach or do not reach.
In our bodies, we find each other.
On our mouths, inner greet,
in our eyes.

A Simple Experiment

When a magnet is
struck by a hammer
the magnetism spills out of
the iron.

The molecules
are jarred,
they are a mob going
in all directions

The magnet is
shockéd back
it is no magnet but
simple iron.

There is no more
of its former
kind of accord
or force.

But if you take
another magnet
and stroke the iron
with this,

it can be
remagnetized
if you stroke it
and stroke it,

stroke it
stroke it,
the molecules
can be given
their tending grace

by a strong magnet
stroking stroking
always in the same direction,
of course.

Along History

Along history, forever
    some woman dancing,
    making shapes on the air;
    forever a man
    riding a good horse,
    sitting the dark horse well,
    his penis erect with
          fantasy

Boys of These Men Full Speed

for Jane Cooper

Boys of these men
  full speed across free,
  my father's boyhood eyes.
  Sail-skating with friends
  bright on Wisconsin ice
  those years away.

Sails strung across their backs
  boys racing toward
  fierce bitter middle-age
  in the great glitter of
  corrupted cities.
  Father, your dark mouth
  speaking its rancor.

Alive not yet, the girl
  I would become
  stares at that ice
  stippled with skaters,
  a story you tell.

Boys of those men
  call across winter
  where I stand and shake,
woman of that girl.

All the Little Animals

"You are not pregnant," said the man
with the probe and the white white coat;
"Yes she is," said all the little animals.
Then the great gynecologist examined. "You are not now,
   and I doubt that you ever have been," he said with
   authority.
"Test me again." He looked at his nurse and shrugged.
"Yes she is," said all the little animals, and laid down their
   lives for my son and me.

Twenty-one years later, my son a grown man and far away
   at the other ocean,
I hear them : "Yes you are," say all the little animals.
I see them, they move in great jumping procession through
   my waking hours,
those frogs and rabbits look at me with their round eyes,
   they kick powerfully with their strong hind legs,
they lay down their lives in silence,
all the rabbits saying Yes, all the frogs saying Yes,
in the face of all men and all institutions,
all the doctors, all the parents, all the worldly friends, all the
   psychiatrists, all the abortionists, all the lawyers.
The little animals whom I bless and praise and thank forever,
they are part of my living,
go leap through my waking and my sleep, go leap through
   my life and my birth-giving and my death,

go leap through my dreams,
and my son's life
and whatever streams from him.

Next

after Charles Morice

Come : you are the one chosen, by them, to serve them.
Now, in the evening of L'Amour and La Mort.
Come : you are the one chosen, by them, to love them.

. . . The child perceives and the cycles are fulfilled.
Man's dead.   Dead never to be reborn.
The Islands and Waters serve another lord,
New, better.   His eyes are the flowering of light.
He is beautiful.   The child smiles at him in his tears.

Two Years

Two years of my sister's bitter illness;
the wind whips the river of her last spring.
I have burned the beans again.

Iris

i

Middle of May, when the iris blows,
blue below blue, the bearded patriarch-
face on the green flute body of a boy
Poseidon   torso of Eros
blue
sky below sea
day over daybreak violet behind twilight
the May iris
midnight on midday

ii

Something is over and under this deep blue.
Over and under this movement, *etwas*
before and after, *alguna cosa*
blue before blue
is it
     perhaps
          death?
That may be the wrong word.

The iris stands in the light.

iii

Death is here, death is guarded by swords.
No. By shapes of swords
flicker of green leaves
under all the speaking and crying
shadowing the words the eyes   here they all die
racing withering   blue evening
my sister death the iris
stands clear in light.

iv

In the water-cave
ferocious needles of teeth
the green morays
in blue water   rays
a maleficence   ribbon of green   the flat look of
eyes staring   fatal mouth staring
the rippling potent force
curving into any hole
death finding his way.

v

Depth of petals, May iris
transparent   infinitely deep they are

petal-thin   with light behind them
and you, death,
and you
behind them
blue under blue.
What I cannot say
in adequate music
something being born
transparency   blue of
light standing on light
this stalk of
(among mortal petals-and-leaves)
light

II Orange and Grape

Ballad of Orange and Grape

After you finish your work
after you do your day
after you've read your reading
after you've written your say —
you go down the street to the hot dog stand,
one block down and across the way.
On a blistering afternoon in East Harlem in the twentieth
century.

Most of the windows are boarded up,
the rats run out of a sack —
sticking out of the crummy garage
one shiny long Cadillac;
at the glass door of the drug-addiction center,
a man who'd like to break your back.
But here's a brown woman with a little girl dressed in rose
and pink, too.

Frankfurters frankfurters sizzle on the steel
where the hot-dog-man leans —
nothing else on the counter
but the usual two machines,
the grape one, empty, and the orange one, empty,
I face him in between.
A black boy comes along, looks at the hot dogs, goes on
walking.

I watch the man as he stands and pours
in the familiar shape
bright purple in the one marked ORANGE
orange in the one marked GRAPE,
the grape drink in the machine marked ORANGE
and orange drink in the GRAPE.
Just the one word large and clear, unmistakeable, on each
    machine.

I ask him : How can we go on reading
and make sense out of what we read?   —
How can they write and believe what they're writing,
the young ones across the street,
while you go on pouring grape into ORANGE
and orange into the one marked GRAPE —?
(How are we going to believe what we read and we write
    and we hear and we say and we do?)

He looks at the two machines and he smiles
and he shrugs and smiles and pours again.
It could be violence and nonviolence
it could be white and black   women and men
it could be war and peace or any
binary system, love and hate, enemy, friend.
Yes and no, be and not-be, what we do and what we don't
    do.

On a corner in East Harlem
garbage, reading, a deep smile, rape,
forgetfulness, a hot street of murder,

misery, withered hope,
a man keeps pouring grape into ORANGE
and orange into the one marked GRAPE,
pouring orange into GRAPE and grape into ORANGE forever.

Rock Flow, River Mix

Flickering
in the buildings
they dance now
hip   face   and knee
dances I hunted for
when at nineteen
I stood at the river
here, the Hudson
hunting for Africa —
something rumored
caught, poured in shadow and light
face of ecstasy
on film
swivel neck, eternal smile
suffer the night
water flows down
to
today
black theatre, road dusted with light
streaking down over our heads
setting before us, around us
sound track
image track

Martin Luther King, Malcolm X

Bleeding of the mountains
the noon bleeding
he is shot through the voice
all things being broken

The moon returning in her blood
looks down   grows white
loses color
and blazes

. . . and the near star gone   —

voices of cities
drumming in the moon

bleeding of my right hand
my black voice bleeding

Looking

Battles whose names I do not know
Weapons whose wish they dare not teach
Wars whose need they will not show
Tear us tear us each from each,
O my dear
Great sun and daily touch.
Fallen beside a river in Europe,
Burned to grey ash in Africa,
Lain down in the California jail,
O my dear,
Great sun and daily touch.

Flaming in Asia today.

I saw you stare out over Canada
As I stare over the Hudson River.

Don Baty, the draft resister

I Muriel stood at the altar-table
The young man Don Baty stood with us
I Muriel fell away in me
in dread but in a welcoming
I am Don Baty then I said
before the blue-coated police
ever entered and took him.

I am Don Baty, say we all
we eat our bread, we drink our wine.
Our heritance has come, we know,
your arrest is mine. Yes.
Beethoven saying Amen Amen Amen Amen Amen
and all a singing, earth and eyes,
strong and weaponless.

There is a pounding at the door;
now we bring our lives entire.
I am Don Baty. My dear, my dear,
in a kind of welcoming,
here we meet, here we bring
ourselves. They pound on the wall of time.
The newborn are with us singing.

Te Hanh : Long-Ago Garden

The Vietnamese poet Te Hanh (1921–)
was born in the South, was in the Resistance
and in jail. He is now in Hanoi. His 4 books
of poems are Adolescence, South Heart, To
North Vietnam, Wave Song. He is one of
the foremost poets of Vietnam.

The long-ago garden is green deepened on green
Day after day our mother's hair, whiter
We are all far away, each at our work
When do we return to the long-ago garden?

We are a shining day following rain
Like the sun like the moon
The morning star, evening star, they never cross over
When will we go back to the long-ago garden?

We are summer lotus, autumn chrysanthemum,
Ripe tenth-month fig, and fifth-month dragon-eye*
You followed the eighth-month migratory birds
Third month, I left with those who crossed over

You went back into the house one day in spring
I was out picking guava, Mother said
You looked up at the tree-top, where the wind blew through
The leaves touched; lips, speaking my name

When I returned one summer day,
You were at the well washing clothes, Mother said

---

* Dragon's eye, longan, related to the lichee
nut, is the fruit of the tree *Euphoria longana.*

[52

I looked in the pure deep water past the well-rim
Saw only the surface and myself, alone

The long-ago garden is green deepened on green
Day after day our mother's hair, whiter
We are all far away, each at our work
When will we return to the long-ago garden?

Fields Where We Slept

Fields where we slept
Lie underwater now
Clay meadows of nightmare
Beneath the shallow wave.

A tremor of speech
On all lips and all mirrors,
Pink sweater and tornado
Act out the spiral dawn.

South lies evocative
On one fine Negro mouth.
Play of silver in streams
Half lake under.

High on the unplowed red
And waterweeds respond
Where Sheriff Fever
Ordered me to trial,

Where once hatred and fear
Touched me the branch of death,
I may float waves of making
Hung above my lost field.

Remember they say and Incarnatus Est,
The fire-tailed waves, never forget the eyes
Of the distorted jailers or their kindness
Even while they were torturing Mr. Crystal.

Psalms awake and asleep, remember the manmade
Lake where those barren treecrowns rode.
Where air of curses hung, keel of my calm
Rides our created tide.

Welcome from War

The woman to the man :
What is that on your hands?
It is also on my hands.

What is that in your eyes?
You see it in my eyes, do you?

Is your sex intact? Is mine?
Can it be about life now?

You went out to war.
War came over our house.

Our bed is not the same.
We will set about beginnings.

I kiss your hands, I kiss your eyes,
I kiss your sex.

I will kiss, I will bless
all the beginnings.

Facing Sentencing

Children remembering sadness grieve, they grieve.
But sadness is not so terrible.   Children
Grown old speak of fear saying, we are to
Fear only this fear itself.   But fear is not to be so feared.
Numbness is.   To stand before my judge
Not knowing what I mean : to walk up
To him, my judge, and back to nobody
For the courtroom is almost empty, the world
Is almost silent, and suppose we did not know
This power to fall into each other's eyes
And say We love; and say We know each other
And say among silence We will help stop this war.

Secrets of American Civilization

for Staughton Lynd

Jefferson spoke of freedom but he held slaves.
Were ten of them his sons by black women?
Did he sell them? or was his land their graves?
Do we asking our questions become more human?

Are our lives the parable which, living,
We all have, we all know, we all can move?
Then they said : The earth belongs to the living,
We refuse allegiance, we resign office, and we love.

They are writing at their desks, the thinking fathers,
They do not recognize their live sons' faces;
Slave and slaveholder they are chained together
And one is ancestor and one is child.
Escape the birthplace; walk into the world
Refusing to be either slave or slaveholder.

Wherever

Wherever
we walk
we will make

Wherever
we protest
we will go planting

Make poems
seed grass
feed a child growing
build a house
Whatever we stand against
We will stand feeding and seeding

Wherever
I walk
I will make

Bringing

Bringing their life   these young
bringing their life   rise from their wakings
bringing their life   come to a place
where they make their gifts

The grapes of life of death   of transformation
round they hang at hand   desires   like
   peace
or seed of revolutions that make all things new
and must be lived out, washed in rivers, and themselves
   made new
and bringing their life   the young   they reach
in their griefs   their mistakes   their discovering
bringing their life   they touch   they take
bringing their life   they come to a place

It is raining fire   they are bringing their life
their sex speaks for them   their ideas all speak
their acts arrive   bringing their life entire
They resist a system of wars and rewards
They offer their open faces   they offer their bodies
They offer their hands   bringing their life entire
They offer their life   they are their own gifts
Make life   resist   resist   make life
Bringing their life entire   they come to this moment
Bringing their life entire   they come to this place

[60

Two Sonnets

A LOUIS SONNET

for Louis Untermeyer, his 80th birthday

The jokes, the feuds, the puns, the punishments,
This traditional man being brave, going in grace,
Finding the structure of lives more than perfected line;
The forms of poetry are his time and space.
He's quirky, he rhymes like daily life; light wine
Is all his flavor, till fierce reverence
Turns delicatessen into delicatesse —
The man who anthologizes experience.

He is anthologized; like a wave of the sea
He is here, he is there, he changes;   impossibly,
He is blue surface, green suspended, the dark deep notes.
A stain of brilliance spreading upward floats
In luminous air; we are luminous, he makes us be
The jokes of Job and Heine's anecdotes.

TO BE A JEW IN THE TWENTIETH CENTURY

To be a Jew in the twentieth century
Is to be offered a gift.   If you refuse,
Wishing to be invisible, you choose
Death of the spirit, the stone insanity.
Accepting, take full life, full agonies:
Your evening deep in labyrinthine blood
Of those who resist, fail and resist; and God
Reduced to a hostage among hostages.

The gift is torment.   Not alone the still
Torture, isolation; or torture of the flesh.
That may come also.   But the accepting wish,
The whole and fertile spirit as guarantee
For every human freedom, suffering to be free,
Daring to live for the impossible.

After Melville

for Bett and Walter Bezanson

I

The sea-coast looks at the sea, and the cities pour.
The sea pours embassies of music : murder-sonata, birth-
    sonata,
the seashore celebrates the deep ocean.

Ocean dreaming all day all night of mountains
lifts a forehead to the wakes of stars;
one star dives into a still circle : birth, known to all.

A shore of the sea, one man as the shore of the sea;
one young man lying out over configurations of water
never two wave-patterns the same, never two same
    dreamings.

He writes these actualities, these dreamings,
transformed into themselves, his acts, his islands,
his animals ourselves within his full man's hand.

Bitter contempt and bitter poverty,
Judaean desert of our life, being locked
in white in black, a lock of essences.

Not graves not ocean but ourselves tonight
swing in his knowledge, his living and its wake,
travelling in the sea that goes pouring, dreaming

[63

where we flash in our lifetime wave, these breathing shallows
of a shore that looks at the deep land, this island
that looks forever at the sea; deep sexual sea
that breathes one man at the shoreline of emergence.
He is the sea we carry to our star.

II

They come into our lives, Melville and Whitman who
ran contradictions of cities and the one-sparing sea
held in the long male arms — Identify.

They enter our evenings speaking—Melville and Crane
taking the wars of our parentage, silence and smoke,
tearing the live man open till we wake.

Emily Dickinson, Melville in our breathing,
isolate among powers, telling us the sea
and the slow dance of the absence of the sea.

Hawthorne whose forehead knew the revelation—
how can we receive the vision at noonday?
Move with the revelation?   Move away?

More violent than Melville   diving the sea deeper
no man has ever gone.   He swims our world
violence and dream safe only in full danger.

Revealing us, who are his afterlife.

III

A woman looks at the sea.
    Woman in whose waiting is held ocean
    faces the other sea where his life drowns and is saved,
    recurrent singing, the reborn wave.

A man looking into the sea.
    He sails, he swims among the opposites,
    diving, making a life among many unknowns,
    he takes for his knowledge the future wake of stars.

The sea looking and not looking.
    Among the old enemies, a transparent lake.
    Wars of the sea and land, wars of air;   space;
    against the corroded wars and sources of wars, a lake
        of being born.

A man and a woman look into each other.
    One man giving us forever the grapes of the sea.
    Gives us marriage; gives us suicide and birth; he drowns
    for the sake of our look into each other's body and life.
    Allowing the great life : sex, time, the feeding powers.
    He is part of our look into each other's face.

The Writer

for Isaac Bashevis Singer

His tears fell from his veins
They spoke for six million
From his veins all their blood.
He told his stories.
But noone spoke this language
Noone knew this music.

His music went into all people
Not knowing this language.
It ran through their bodies
And they began to take his words
Everyone the tears
Everyone the veins
But everyone said
Noone spoke this language.

Gradus ad Parnassum

Oh I know
If I'd practised the piano
I'd never be so low
As I now am

Where's Sylvia Beerman?
Married, rich and cool
In New Rochelle
She was nobody's fool,

She didn't write in verse
She hardly wrote at all
She rose she didn't fall
She never gave a damn

But got up early
To practise Gradus
Ad Parnassum — she
Feels fine. I know.

From a Play : Publisher's Song

I lie in the bath and I contemplate the toilet-paper:
Scottissue, 1000 sheets —
    What a lot of pissin and shittin,
    What a lot of pissin and shittin,
Enough for the poems of Shelley and Keats —
All the poems of Shelley and Keats.

In the Night the Sound Woke Us

In the night the sound woke us.
We went up to the deck.
Brightness of brightness in the black night.
The ship standing still, her hold wide open.
Light shining orange on the lumber
her cargo, fresh strong-smelling wood.
A tall elder sailor standing at the winches,
his arms still, down; not seeming to move,
his hands hidden behind
black leather balcony.
The silver-hair tall sailor, stern and serene his face
turning from side to side.
The winches fell and rose with the newborn wood.
Orange and blazing in the lights it rose.
Vancouver straits, a northern midnight.
Delivered from death I stood awake
seeing it brought to the cool shining air.
O death, skillful, at night, in the bright light
bringing to birth.

Over my head
I see it in the air.

In the Underworld

I go a road
among the upturned
faces in their colors
to the great arch
of a theatre stage

I the high queen
starting in the air
far above my head
royal of the crown
I the tower
go through the wide arch
proscenium queen

✿

The arch shuts down like December
very small all about me
the entrance to this country

✿

Many whispers in the quick dark
Fingers in swarms, breath is busy,
they have reached above my head

and taken off my crown
I go and I go
I have been searching
since the light of all mornings

I remember only a pale brightness
and no more.　　What do I remember?
I no longer

They have reached to my jewels
green in this cave, that one, iceberg the blue,
whirled into diamond
in the deep dark taken.

I move into thicker dark,
moss, earth-smell, wet coal.
Their hands are on my stiff robe.
I walk out of my robe.

At my surfaces
they unfasten my dress of softness.
Naked the naked wind
of the underworld.

Rankness at my breasts,
over my flank
giggle and stink
They have taken little knives
my skin lifts off
I go in pain-colored black
trying to find

I walk into their asking
Where is he
they sing on one note
Your lord memory
He your delight
I cannot hear their music
it scrapes along my muscles
they make my flesh go
among the gusts and whispers
they take off my eyes
my lips no more
the delicate fierce places
of identity
everywhere
taken

I, despoiled and clacking
walk, a chain of bones
into the boneyard dark.
One by one.
Something
reaches for my bones.

✼

Something walks here
a little breath in hell
without its ghost.
A breath after nothing.

Gone.
Nothing turns the place
where perceiving was
from side to side.
There is no place.   It has dissolved.
The lowest point, back there, has slid away.

✣

— What are you working on?
— Istar in the underworld.
— Baby, you are in trouble.

✣

What calls her?
The body of a woman alive
but at the point of death,
the very old body lying there riddled with life,
gone, gasping at pain,
fighting for words
fighting for breath.
One clear breast looks up out of this gone body
young, the white clear light of this breast
speaks across distance

✣

Remember is
come back.
Remember is
Who is here?
I am here.

✿

At the pit of the underworld
something flickers in her
without anything

✿

Now I remember love
who has set my being on me,
who permits me move
into all being,
who puts on me perceiving
and my bones
in a live chain
and my flesh that perceives
and acts
and my acknowledging skin
my underdress, my dress
and my robe
the jewels of the world
I touch and find

[74

— I know him and I know
　　the breast speaking
　　out of a gone woman
　　across distances

And my crown a tower.

A voice saying　:　She went in a queen,
　　　　　　　　　she died and came out,
　　　　　　　　　goddess.

All our faces in their colors
　　staring at the
　　arch of this world.

The breast smiles : Do not
　　think you are invulnerable!
The breast smiles : Do not
　　think you are immortal!

Afterwards

We are the antlers of that white animal
That great white animal
Asleep under the sea
He forgets and dreams so deep he does not
Know his whiteness in the sea-black
Among the plants of night.
His antlers have legs and arms.   Our heads
together being joined
Journey tonight, dreamed in his ocean.

Where we lie afterwards, smoke of our dreams
Goes coiling up, a plant in the dark room.
You were a young boy, you sang in the Polish woods
Limping away away.   I in this city, held
In a dream of children.   Some mythic animal
Rises now, flies up, white from the sea-floor.
In all our death, the glow behind his eyes
Speaks under all knowing : our lives burn.

Flying There: Hanoi

I thought I was going to the poets, but I am
  going to the children.
I thought I was going to the children, but I am
  going to the women.
I thought I was going to the women, but I am going
  to the fighters.
I thought I was going to the fighters, but I am
  going to the men and women who are inventing peace.
I thought I was going to the inventors of peace,
  but I am going to the poets.
My life is flying to your life.

It Is There

Yes, it is there, the city full of music,
Flute music, sounds of children, voices of poets,
The unknown bird in his long call.   The bells of peace.
Essential peace, it sounds across the water
In the long parks where the lovers are walking,
Along the lake with its island and pagoda,
And a boy learning to fish.   His father threads the line.
Essential peace, it sounds and it stills.   Cockcrow.
It is there, the human place.

On what does it depend, this music, the children's games?
A long tradition of rest? Meditation? What peace is so
     profound
That it can reach all habitants, all children,
The eyes at worship, the shattered in hospitals?
All voyagers?
                    Meditation, yes; but within a tension
Of long resistance to all invasion, all seduction of hate.
Generations of holding to resistance; and within this
     resistance
Fluid change that can respond, that can show the children
A long future of finding, of responsibility; change within
Change and tension of sharing consciousness
Village to city, city to village, person to person entire
With unchanging cockcrow and unchanging endurance
Under the
               skies of war.

The Running of the Grunion

for Denise Levertov and Mitchell Goodman

1

Launching themselves
beating silver
on that precise
moment of tide & moon.

Exact in act
outer limit
stranded on high sand.
With an arched back he
digs their bed
she under him
releases he
fertilizes and
with back arched
covers (sand)
the gleam spawn.

On the lit beach
the hunt begins:
silver buckets.
People run down
for the huge catch.
Pulsing on sand
countless silver.

Highest wave
stretches
among the hunt.
A few of the fish
are washed to sea.

The spawn enclosed
in high sand
rhythms of hot & cool;
a full moon later
the wave foams over;
young grunion
wash to ocean.

Eleven later,
mature, silver,
they return.

People with pails.

II

Sand nailed down
by beating silver
nailed
by live nails

Sand is not crucified
only people
only animals

III

These creatures
cruciform.
To make life.

In the act of life
murder
people with pails

IV

Silver
on silver
birth
and
murder

Not birth
conception

V

Seawave
moon
seasand
at the moment of life

They throw themselves
million silver
upon making

Whether or not
people with pails

Sacred Lake

some flushed-earth-color pueblo
holding the long-light sunset
shadows go into this ground
the mountain lifting the lake
in an orante gesture
like the men
in their white shirt-sleeves
in the basement of the Planetarium
the mailman the policeman the highschool-teacher
these winter evenings   making their own telescopes
they hold them up to test them the only way
against a ray of light in a gesture of offering.

This long wide gorge and mesa make the gesture
holding each man up against sunset light
and holding Blue Lake up.

▌▌▌ Northern Poems

*Eskimo Songs translated by Paul Radin
and Muriel Rukeyser*

Songs of the Barren Grounds

1. THE OLD DAYS

Song-calling,
Breathing deep, my heart laboring,
Calling the song.
Hearing the news:
Faraway villages in their
Terrible fishing seasons,
Breathing deep and
Calling the song;
Come down, song.
Now I forget
The laboring breast,
I remember the old days:
My strength, butchering
Caribou bulls,
Calling the song —
I call the song.
Three bulls butchered
While the sun climbed morning —
I call the song
Breathing deep
— Aya ayee —
Calling the song.

2. INLAND, AWAY

Inland, away
Grieving I know I
Shall not leave again
This bench, this place.
Wanderwishing troubles me:
Going inland, going away.
My thoughts keep playing with a thing that seems
Animal flesh
And yet I know I
Shall not leave again
This bench, this place.
Feeling the old wish to go
Inland, away.
Here I am, I —
Never again to go out with the rest.
I was the one who shot them down, both:
The widespread antlers, old caribou,
And the young one too.
Once
When heaven-twilight
Lay over the land —
Going inland, going away.
— Aya, yee, ya. —
All this, unforgotten,
All my fantasy.
That hunting, and my fortunes,

That caribou and calf,
While all the earth
Whitened with snow.
Inlandaway.
Inlandaway.

3. I'M HERE AGAIN

I'm here again —
What's the matter?   Want to say something?
Something I heard told around:
I'm here to tell,
I'm here to tell,
I'm here to tell
How you and your
Uncle's
Younger sister
Went to bed.
Just at the coming of the great springtime.
I'm here to tell,
I'm here to tell,
I'm here to tell,
You sure have been fucking, you two.
What do you say now?   How about it?
"Open your legs now, nice and wide!"
When you got there, hard,
How was she?
I'm here again.
Here I am.

4. NOT MUCH GOOD

I'm not much good at any of this.
Is the song too long, is the song too long?
He wanted his sister, he did he did —
That's what they said that people said.
Well you rascal, you rascal you.
Think I'd sing a pack of lies,
Lies about a fellow who never
Made a pass at his little sister?
Well you rascal, you rascal you —
Know what they said, they said you did?
Came sneaking in to your little sister,
Sneaked in to screw your little sister.
Know what she asked you?
"Well, what you doing?"
Pretty silly, you looked —
Sneaking in, to screw his sister!
. . . . To show him up
I'm singing this song.

5. MY BREATH

A song I sing, strong I sing,
Helpless as my own child, ever since last fall.

My house and my wife, I wish they were gone.
With me, she's with a worthless man;
Her man should be strong as winter ice.
I am bedridden and
I wish she were gone.

Do we know ourselves?

Beasts of the hunt!   Can I remember one?
Faintly remembering the polar bear,
White back high, head lowered, charging,
Sure he was the one male there,
Full speed at me.

Had me down again and again—
He didn't lie over me, he went away.
Hadn't expected another male there
At the edge of the ice-floe
He knew who he was, he rested.

I can never forget the fjord-seal
On the sea ice;   I killed it early
When my comrades, my land-sharers

Were just waking.
Reaching the breathing-hole,
I discovered it,
And then I was standing over the hole   —
I hadn't scratched the ice, the firm ice,
And the bear hooked under   —
It heard me, that good seal, that cunning seal.
And just tasting my disappointment if I lost it
I caught it with my harpoon head!

My house and wife are here.
I have no oil for her lamp and spring has come,
Dawn gives way to dawn;   when will I be well?
My house;   my wife, by neighbors
Clothed, by charity
Eating meat.
Not my providing; when will I be well?

Do we know ourselves?
Little you know of yourself,
Dawn giving way to dawn.

Orpingalik

I Recognize This Song

I recognize this little song   —
It's a fellow-being.
Sure, I should be ashamed
Of the child I carried,
I've heard
The neighbors talking   —
Sure, I should be ashamed
Because his mother
Wasn't as pure
As the pure blue sky;
I got what was coming;
Gossip will teach him
And finish his schooling.
Sure, I should be ashamed
The child I love won't ever take care of me.
When others go hunting
Out on the flat ice
And far behind, people
Stand looking at them
A person feels envy!
I've just remembered
Once in wintertime
At Cross-Eye Island, breaking camp,
The weather was   —   Down there
Footsteps creaked faintly in the snow,
Sinking.   I followed close, like a tame animal.

Oh, that's the way to be.
But when the message came
Of murder done by my son
I staggered.   I could not keep my foothold.

The Black Ones, the Great Ones

After the black ones!
Racing the great ones!
Over the plain-flowers
With all my strength.
Running breakneck
Forever after
Horizon-animals.
Obsessed!   They're growing
Out of the ground!
The giants!   I shot them,
The great ones, the black ones,
Faraway
In the summer-hunting.

Trout Fishing

Well, I'm back again
To this song —
Back again, standing over
My old fishing-place.
And I'm not one who's good at going back,
A hook waiting for trout.
Upstream and up the stream.
There aren't any trout around here
Unless you wait.
I keep saying There aren't many trout this year.
There are those I eat and those I don't wait for
Because I give up so soon.
Upstream and up the stream;
Well, and it's glorious
On snowy ice-surfaces
Walking and walking.
I can't even go errands —
I, a falling-down old man.
Everything else is fine. . . .
I cannot even make my difficult song,
For easy birdsong is not given to me,
Even though I turn to it again,
And I'm not one who's good at going back.

O, difficult things!   And I want everything.

Ikinilik

How Lovely It Is

How lovely it is to
Put a little song together.
Many of mine fail, yes they do.
How lovely it all is,
But me, I seldom burn with luck,
Hunting across the ice, alas.
How lovely it all is
To wish and bring it through.
But again and again
My wishes slip away!
How very hard, how very hard it all is, yes, alas.

Ikinilik

The Word-Fisher

I know what I want in my words
But it will not turn into song
And it's not worth the listening!
To make my song
Really good listening,
That's pretty hard —
But listen : Some clumsy song . . .
Is in the making . . .
And is made!

Stroking Songs

A GIRL FOR A BOY—STROKING SONG

It's still my little big "big brother," isn't it?
The one I wanted to make new, isn't it?
The one I didn't do such a good job on, isn't it?

I'm going to have to prime my tool again,
There'll have to be work done in the bag.
I didn't do a good job, that's what the man says now.

THE BABY ON THE MOUNTAIN—STROKING SONG

Up against the mountain-side
The little early-born —
No stopping-place, no hiding-place
Pushing it out, pushing it out. —

White skin, furless skin,
Great skin of harbor seal,
Great skin, hanging soft,
Great skin hanging free.

Roughened by the east wind
Pushing pushing,
I'm sorry, it's only
The southern winds.

This is the way we
This is the way we open it,
This is the way we
Make it hard.

This is the way we
Stroke the baby,
Stroking the baby's
Parts.

This is the way of the baby's groin,
This is the way the baby'll marry,
A real man with a fine one,
A real man with a darling one.

Stroking, stroking, stroke the baby.

THE WIPING MOSS FROM THE RUINS

Running to me —
My wiping moss —
Breakneck from the ruined house.

Well, a nipple full of milk
And a fine pot-stone, yes,
Welcome as the light of spring,
Welcome as a seal in spring!

Well, the milk of the nipple, listen,
Listen : hear them shout
Where is that milk?
All the way up from Ipsetaleq.

Then what, what, what's the matter?
Pinch you, pinch you, pinch your crotch.
Falling all over yourself, darling.

Stroking Songs, Childhood Songs

BEING BORN

She was unloaded and delivered to us, glory be!
Unloaded from her mother, the little one, delivered,
And we all say Glory Be!

SHOOTING STAR

You star up there,
Starer up there,
Your fingers up there
Not holding very tight,
Not catching — not tight —
And falling downwards,
Downwards and falling falling
Downward down the night.

IV Breaking Open

Breaking Open

I come into the room   The room stands waiting
river   books   flowers   you are far away
black river   a language just forgotten
traveling blaze of light   dreams of endurance
racing into this moment   outstretched faces
and you are far away
                              The stars cross over
fire-flood   extremes of singing
filth and corrupted promises   my river
A white triangle of need
                              my reflected face
laced with a black triangle   of need

Naked among the silent of my own time
and Zig Zag Zag that last letter
     of a secret or forgotten alphabet
     shaped like our own last letter but it means
Something in our experience you do not know
When will it open open opening
River-watching all night
                              will the river
swing open we are Asia and New York
Bombs, roaches, mutilation   River-watching

✿

Looking out at the river
the city-flow seen as river
the flow seen as a flow of possibility
and I too to that sea.

✹

Summer repetitive. The machine screaming
Beating outside, on the corrupted
Waterfront.
On my good days it appears digging
And building,
On others, its monstrous word
Says on one note Gone, killed, laid waste.

The whole thing — waterfront, war, city,
        sons, daughters, me —
Must be re-imagined.
Sun on the orange-red roof.

❈

Walking into the elevator at Westbeth
Yelling in the empty stainless-steel
Room like the room of this tormented year.
Like the year
The metal nor absorbs nor reflects
My yelling.
My pulled face looks at me
From the steel walls.

✿

And then we go to Washington as if it were
Jerusalem;
and then we present our petition, clearly,
rightfully;
and then some of us walk away;
and then do others of us stay;
and some of us lie gravely down
on that cool mosaic floor,
the Senate.
Washington! Your bombs rain down!
I mourn, I lie down, I grieve.

✵

Written on the plane:

The conviction that what is meant by the unconscious is the same as what is meant by history. The collective unconscious is the living history brought to the present in consciousness, waking or sleeping. The personal "unconscious" is the personal history. This is an identity.
We will now explore further ways of reaching our lives, the new world. My own life, yours; this earth, this moon, this system, the "space" we share, which is consciousness.

Turbulence of air now. A pause of nine minutes.

✼

Written on the plane. After turbulence:

The movement of life : to live more fully in the present. This movement includes the work of bringing this history to "light" and understanding. The "unconscious" of the race, and its traces in art and in social structure and "inventions" — these are our inheritance. In facing history, we look at each other, and in facing our entire personal life, we look at each other.

I want to break open. On the plane, a white cloud seen through rainbow. The rainbow is, optically, on the glass of the window.

✻

The jury said Guilty, Guilty, Guilty,
Guilty, Guilty.   Each closed face.
I see myself in the river-window.   River
Slow going to its sea.
An old, crushed, perverse, waiting,
In loss, in dread, dead tree.

❋

COLUMBUS

Inner greet.   Greenberg said it,
Even the tallest man needs inner greet.
This is the great word
brought back, in swinging seas.   The new world.

*

End of summer.
Dark-red butterflies on the river
Dark-orange butterflies in the city.
The young men still going to war
Or away from war, to the prisons, to other countries.
To the high cold mountains, to the source of the river,
  I too go,
Deeper into this room.

*

A dream remembered only in other dreams.
The voice saying:
All you dreaded as a child
Came to pass in storms of light;
All you dreaded as a girl
Falls and falls in avalanche —
Dread and the dream of love will make
All that time and men may build,
All that women dance and make.
They become you.   Your own face
Dances through the night and day,
Leading your body into this
Body-led dance, its mysteries.
Answer me.   Dance my dance.

✲

River-watching from the big Westbeth windows:
Powerful miles of Hudson, an east-blowing wind
All the way to Asia.
No.   Lost in our breath,
Sobbing, lost, alone.   The river darkens.
Black flow, bronze lights, white lights.
Something must answer that light, that dark.
Love,
The door opens, you walk in.

✻

The old man said, "The introversion of war
Is the main task of our time."
Now it makes its poem, when the sky stops killing.
I try to turn my acts inward and deeper.
Almost a poem.   If it splash outside,
All right.
My teacher says, "Go deeper."
The day when the salmon-colored flowers
Open.
I will essay.   Go deeper.

Make my poem.

✲

Going to prison. The clang of the steel door.
It is my choice. But the steel door does clang.
The introversion of this act
Past its seeming, past all thought of effect,
Until it is something like
Writing a poem in my silent room.

*

In prison, the thick air,
still, loaded, heat on heat.
Around your throat
for the doors are locks,
the windows are locked doors,
the hot smell locked around us,
the machine shouting at us,
trying to sell us meat and carpets.
In prison, the prisoners,
all of us, all the objects,
chairs, cots, mops, tables.
Only the young cat.
He does not know he is locked in.

✢

In prison, the prisoners.
One black girl, 19 years.
She has killed her child
and she grieves, she grieves.
She crosses to my bed.
"What do *Free* mean?"
I look at her.
"You don't understand English."
"Yes, I understand English."
"What do *Free* mean?"

✿

In prison a
brown paper bag
I put it beside my cot.
All my things.
Comb, notebook, underwear,
letterpaper, toothbrush, book.
I am rich —
they have given me another toothbrush.
The guard saying:
"You'll find people share here."

✿

Photos, more precise than any face can be.
    The broken static moment, life never by
    any eye seen.

                    ❋   ❋   ❋

My contradictions set me tasks, errands.

                    ❋   ❋   ❋

This I know:
What I reap, that shall I sow.

                    ❋

How we live:
I look into my face in the square glass.
Under it, a bright flow of cold water.
At once, a strong arrangement of presences:
I am holding a small glass
under the little flow
at Fern Spring, among the western forest.
A cool flaw among the silence.
The taste of the waterfall.

*

Some rare battered she-poet, old girl in the Village
racketing home past low buildings some freezing night,
come face to face with that broad roiling river.
Nothing buried in her but is lit and transformed.

✼

BURNING THE DREAMS

on a spring morning of young wood, green wood
it will not burn, but the dreams burn.
My hands have ashes on them.
They fear it
and so they destroy the nearest things.

✷

DEATH AND THE DANCER

Running from death
throwing his teeth at the ghost
dipping into his belly, staving off death with a throw
tearing his brains out, throwing them at Death
death-baby is being born
scythe clock and banner come
trumpet of bone   and drum made of something   —
the callous-handed goddess
her kiss is resurrection

✿

RATIONAL MAN

The marker at Auschwitz
The scientists torturing male genitals
The learned scientists, they torture female genitals
The 3-year-old girl, what she did to her kitten
The collar made of leather for drowning a man in his chair
The scatter-bomb with the nails that drive into the brain
The thread through the young man's splendid penis
The babies in flames.   The thrust
Infected reptile dead in the live wombs of girls
We did not know we were insane.
We do not know we are insane.
We say to them : you are insane
Anything you can imagine
    on punishable drugs, or calm and young
    with a fever of 105, or on your knees,
    with the word of Hanoi bombed
    with the legless boy in Bach Mai
    with the sons of man torn by man
Rational man has done.

Mercy, Lord.   On every living life.

✿

In tall whirlpools of mirrors
Unshapen body and face
middle of the depth
of a night that will not turn
the unshapen all night
trying for form

*

I do and I do.
Life and this under-war.
Deep under protest, make.
For we are makers more.

but touching teaching going
the young and the old
they reach they break they are moving
to make the world

✲

something about desire
something about murder
something about my death
something about madness

something about light
something of breaking open
sing me to sleep and morning
my dreams are all a waking

✿

In the night
wandering room to room of this world
I move by touch
and then something says
let the city pour
the sleep of the beloved
Let the night pour down
all its meanings
Let the images pour
the light is dreaming

✻

THE HOSTAGES

When I stand with these three
My new brothers my new sister
These who bind themselves offering
Hostages to go at a word, hostages
to go deeper here among our own cities
When I look into your faces
Karl, Martin, Andrea.

When I look into your faces
Offered men and women, I can speak,
And I speak openly on the church steps,
At the peace center saying : We affirm
Our closeness forever with the eyes in Asia,
Those who resist the forces we resist.
One more hostage comes forward, his eyes: Joe,
With Karl, Martin, Andrea, me.

And now alone in the river-watching room,
Allen, your voice comes, the deep prophetic word.
And we are one more, Joe, Andrea, Karl, Martin,
Allen, me.   The hostages.   Reaching.   Beginning.

✿

That I looked at them with my living eyes.
That they looked at me with their living eyes.
That we embraced.
That we began to learn each other's language.

It is something like the breaking open of my youth
but unlike too, leading not only to consummation
of the bed and of the edge of the sea.
Although that, surely, also.

But this music is
itself
needing only other selving
It is defeated but a way is open:
transformation

✿

Then came I entire to this moment
process and light
      to discover the country of our waking
breaking open

❉

Notes

Don Baty, a draft resister, took sanctuary in the Washington Square church during the War in Vietnam. Many of us took bread and wine with him and said, "I am Don Baty." When the police came for him and asked, "Who is Don Baty?" everyone said, "I am Don Baty."

The Eskimo poems were translated by Paul Radin and Muriel Rukeyser from texts given by Rasmussen and others. They have been adapted from material in: *The Netsilik Eskimos—Social Life and Spiritual Culture,* by Knud Rasmussen; Gyldendalske Boghandel, Nordisk Forlag, Copenhagen; *Intellectual Culture of the Caribou Eskimos—Iglulik and Caribou Eskimo Texts,* by Knud Rasmussen, same publisher; *The Ammassalik Eskimo II:* Nr. 3, W. Thalbitzer; *Language and Folklore,* C. A. Reitzel, Boghandel, Kobenhaven. The glossary used was *Five Hundred Eskimo Words,* by Kaj Birket-Smith. The last drafts were written in 1973, after the death of Paul Radin, that incomparable man.

"To Be a Jew. . . ." written during World War II, is now included in the new Reform Jewish prayerbook, *The Service of the Heart,* published in London.

"Fields Where We Slept" has its scene in the South, where a manmade lake of the TVA system now lies over some of the land of the Scottsboro Trial actions, the revealing clash of 1933 underwater now. "Remember they say . . ."

In "Searching/Not Searching," the *Kieu* is the epic of Vietnam, H.F.D. is Hallie Flanagan, the director of the Theatre Project (WPA).